FABLESQUE

ANNA MARIA HONG

Tupelo Press

Fablesque
Copyright © 2020 Anna Maria Hong. All rights reserved.

Library of Congress Catalog-in-Publication data available upon request.
ISBN-13: 978-1-946482-34-1

Cover image: *Hungry Plants No. 1*, by Kim So Yeon. Used by kind permission of the artist.

Cover and text design by Kenji Liu.

First paperback edition September 2020

Tupelo Press
P.O. Box 1767
North Adams, Massachusetts 01247
(413) 664-9611 / Fax: (413) 664-9711
editor@tupelopress.org / www.tupelopress.org

Tupelo Press is an award-winning independent literary press that publishes fine fiction, non-fiction, and poetry in books that are a joy to hold as well as read. Tupelo Press is a registered 501(c)(3) non-profit organization, and we rely on public support to carry out our mission of publishing extraordinary work that may be outside the realm of the large commercial publishers. Financial donations are welcome and are tax deductible.

FABLESQUE

ANNA MARIA HONG

CONTENTS

I shall reply then with an example.
Upon meeting others, a savage man
will initially be frightened. Because
of his fear he sees the others as bigger
and stronger than himself. He calls
them giants.

JEAN-JACQUES ROUSSEAU
ESSAY ON THE ORIGIN OF LANGUAGES

1

Be lion-mettled, proud; and take no care who chafes, who frets, or where conspirers are ...

THIRD APPARITION
MACBETH, ACT IV, SCENE I

HELICONIUS MELPOMENE

Not the branch but the dismantling. If

                                          I could have seen the shape of it,

I wouldn't have made the journey.

                                          A coiled tongue

for the pleasure of interpolating. A tripod
to offset my wings.

                                          Predator: know my coloring.
                                          I'll follow you to the ends of folly

like venom in
the bloodstream.

                                     When my father was 19, North Korean
soldiers invaded the South, descending upon Seoul National University where my father
was studying chemistry. The soldiers captured a dozen students and marched them North,
my father among them. The soldiers took the students to a mine to do hard manual labor,
digging mineral from rock in cold, damp caves, giving them thin bowls of rice and rotten
vegetables to eat. After a few weeks of this, my father faked delirium and was sent to the
infirmary from which he escaped along with two other young men from the city.

They made their way through the mountain forests to evade recapture by the soldiers
roaming the villages. They were making their way South to the newly formed border
partitioning the country, but after a few days of scrabbling through the Woods, they
became too hungry, so my father and the other two men entered a village to find food.
Approaching a cottage at the edge of the Woods, they were immediately seized by soldiers,

two men with guns, almost certainly conscripted into the army by force and their own need to eat in the ravaged land.

The young soldiers asked the first of my father's companions two questions: "Where are you from? And where are you going?"

The first boy answered truthfully: "I'm from Seoul. I want to go to my old parents."

The soldier shot him in the head and asked the second man the same questions.

"Where are you from? Where are you going?"

The second man panicked, also blurting out the truth, shaking, "I want to go South to my wife and sons."

The soldier shot him dead too. When they got to my father, he was ready.

"Where are you from? Where are you going?"

My father imitated a Northern rural accent and said, "I'm just a poor Barber trying to go home. I am starving."

The soldiers let him go. My father made it through the mountains—they had not been far from the border—to the still porous DMZ, to the Southern soldiers who directed him across the border to safety, back to the university, to his father and stepmother, and eventually to America and 63 more years of living. To building an importing-exporting business, becoming an expert in the crossing of visible and hidden boundaries. To building a family, to destroying both business and family, mourning the loss of the former, ending up with the latter anyway, his devoted wife, my mother, nursing him through two traumatic brain injuries, his sons by his side, living out the last decades of his life in a suburban twilight of former glamour and glory.

When he told me that tale, one of the few he told me, he relayed it with drama but not much emotion, as if he were recalling a sea monster he'd caught as a boy with just a paperclip and a ball of string.

"And that's why I'm strong," he said. "After that day I never feared anything. Unless someone was pointing a gun at me, I wasn't afraid of anything. Everything else is nothing."

"That's why you're an asshole," I thought. I was about 13. I don't know where we were, if it was in the house my parents would lose in a few years or some other now inhumed place. My middle-aged father's smooth, blankly animated face telling the parable of his own cunning and lack of disabling empathy.

The Viceroy appears almost identical to the Monarch butterfly, emulating its size, shape, and markings to avoid being eaten. The Monarch's diet of milkweed makes it toxic to the birds that would make it their prey.

My father's story has the simplicity of a fairy tale: three brothers, three forks in road, three wishes: one way to proceed. A series of trials followed by the happy ending, though of course, this was just one story in the long braid of tales that would make up my father's life, my mother's, my brothers', and anyone else's his decisions ended up torqueing.

The forest setting. The frightened villagers, then as now, impoverished and terrorized by a ravenous beast. Hunger carving a path through the Woods to the cottage where my father's fate awaited. As does yours. As does mine.

3

MAIDEN

My father died in my sleep. I built the cage; he planted the idea like a mangrove seed.

My father died when I was in the Manticore's castle splashed by the green-gray sea. The sound of incense furring my breast. The Manticore never touched me with anything but his hat and blunt human teeth. He was the mate of my educated choosing. Shunt is the rape of the oil in the seed.

My father was 19 when he ate me. I wasn't born yet, but the idea had to make. *Cardinalis cardinalis.* I have mirrored that intelligence in the tangent of my singing.

                                        Other birds punctuate (our) song.
My father became a red bird after dying: singer-soldier-doctor-door. A better debtor without his body.

                                        To tease the beast out of me
                                        and leave the body blue like the crowns
of babies. Storyteller, sing firmly.

BEAR

The Bear is licking her babies. Born without shape, the babies are smooth, hairless balls of flesh. Formless as dirt, the babies are crying. The mother Bear licks and licks with her wide blue tongue, slicking off the first layer of slime and sleep.

The mother Bear holds one ball in her giant paws. The baby is as big as an acorn, smaller than the Bear's clawed thumb. The Bear eats some of her babies, thinking they are berries. She has been asleep for a long, long time, sleeping alone in her cave all winter. She is, like all animals, periodically starving, her black fur matted with bat droppings and four-month-old honey. She swallows her babies like regret. The survivors squirm in her paws.

The Bear licks off the first skin to reveal another: soft black hair like an Asian baby's. Her tongue is pointed and indiscriminate. Her ideas are rough—not thought so much as the compulsion to clean her mess of offspring, one of which begins to scream, its mouth a brown slit, making a sound only Bears can hear.

The mother Bear drops this baby, flinging it to the ground in one decisive sweep. In that moment the baby becomes a cub, adorable and slightly grown, someone the mother Bear can talk to about her thwarted ambitions, her absent lover, the pain of giving birth during hibernation.

URSUS

... as the Bear enters the dome through his mother's womb and exits through the shaft of an arrow, which has pierced his heart. In between: wild rice, dark blue apples, bowls of greens cooked to warm perfection. The cage of birchwood that he could have broken at any point, but chose not to. The golden chain around his neck, similarly symbolic. His brown fur combed smooth by the village children and oiled by the women. The Orator reciting stories of his enchanted birth and noble lineage, as he drifts off to sleep each night.

                                        No mother after the first week
of life. No other bears in sight. The smell of roasted seal and auk. No promises,
only intimations.

                                    And still
                                    the sudden drop of
                                    recognition—the burst
                                    at the end of the tunnel—the
                                    knowledge transferred

in one
swift
blow.

RABBIT

R is for river and RODENTIA, the rodent formerly known as Cony is making her way to the village, having breakfasted satisfactorily on a tawny sandwich of old bread, lettuce, tomato, and a slice of Swiss cheese.

Skin is what the villagers esteem, so she covers it under long-sleeved gabardine and a broad-brimmed hat. Silver gray, the skin. Beauty hides; neutrality roams.

Though the day is warm, the Rabbit chatters her round cheeks, smelling the mown grass and overriding her desire to pause and eat and pause and eat and pause and eat. She keeps her hat strapped, her gaze firm, striding forward like the hare, whom she likes but doesn't trust. She is afraid of running into the Flemish Giant, largest of all the breeds. She finds the Giant repulsive, a monstrosity of race, though she understands it is not his fault being huge any more than it is hers for possessing coveted skin.

"It's just teleology," she thinks. "The endpoint of domestication." She thinks about domesticity and mastication, as she chews on thought after thought. *Domesticity, a little lawn, white rooms with brown floors cleaned with rags and palm oil, a basket of carrots, and a little gray fence.* The day is golden, perfect as a walnut.

She knows that they are the last of their kind, all of them. Herself, a descendant of Dutch colonists, the punctilious hare, the Flemish abomination with his thighs the size of her head. They are the last of their lines in spite of incessant breeding. The villagers' desire for variety—for skin, shape, and size—is insatiable, but the river has shifted, and all that breeding will bear no seed.

WOLF

The Wolf is in a trap set by the Woodcutter who whittles a sharp stick to plunge in the Wolf's eye. Let's assume this takes place in the savage North, not so savage now in the pleasant blanch of summer. Ferocity resides in the man's shoulder, congested with repetitive work, the motions of a dedicated craftsman. Like a young worm burning through its mother, the Woodcutter would like to eat the Wolf. He would like to roast it after poking out its eyes. The Woodcutter is a shy man, self-conscious about his intentions. He does not want to be seen by the beast when he slits its belly from throat to hole.

The Wolf was entrapped by its cravings—not for the Woodcutter with whom she has no quarrel or interest but for the Woodcutter's beasts: his chickens, his goats, his sheep, the animals of restive living. But the Wolf is not picky. If the Woodcutter had kept monkeys, cockatiels, or Schnauzers, the Wolf would have pursued them too. As it is, the Wolf can no longer pursue anything but her own hunger, which will not be sated, which cannot be whittled away. She did not expect to have such a disgusting death, the Woodcutter's scent her last pure experience.

THE ANTS

I am walking through the corridors of a large, corporate hotel, passing groups of Korean American men in business suits. The light filters starkly through high windows and thick curtains.

A young hapa man wearing wire-rimmed glasses stops me, saying, "Professor H____, how nice to see you here." I don't recognize him, but I assume he's a colleague or a student. I believe we are all here for a wedding. He moves off with his group. I am surprised to be identified. I am traveling alone.

Then, I'm in a hotel room, and I am male, I think, the crotch of my unflattering Sansabelt pants bulge ambiguously, and I am held in place, though I see no binders. I am being eaten by hundreds of ants who tear away at my torso, and as I gaze at my own unfamiliar face through the doorframe, my body appears to be suspended against a blue-gray backdrop, light streaming through nondescript windows.

The estranged face is unmistakably mine and set squarely against the pain, although I am not bleeding. Like Prometheus, I will recover between eatings. When the ants stop, I myself will feast, devouring banquets of roasted fowl, *kalbi,* mutton. Having my insides consumed makes me very hungry.

Soon, I know, the ants will begin anew, eating out my soft middle, as I return to this blue-gray room again and again.

TERMITE

T is for tabloid and all the time in the world,
a tulle twist of time wound round
the pole of infinite delight. The Queen is
the tuning fork in the tenor of time,
resplendent in her distension,
her slick abdomen the color of tea,
pulsing the next iteration. The Queen's abdomen
is an open medium, ejecting every
few seconds, 30,000 eggs per diem. Workers
with their heavy misshapen heads
continuously feed her, climbing the tower
from chamber to light and threat
to refresh the fungus garden,
so that she may eat as she excretes
each child worker or soldier and rarely:
a new Boy King. This is pleasure as
industry. This is life centrifuged to terminal
velocity: consume, fuck in the royal
chamber of public scrutiny, serve
your servant babies.

ANTELOPE

All nerve and no pain make Jane a beaver without a cunt, a sex toupee.

            Pass me the gas in the Mason's bottle
            to rinse
            the conjugal
            out of me.

            I'm a Barbary ape shrunk
            to the depth
            of a candle
            -stick.

Flap that

            dick like a manual
            alphabet. Every anthem
            is a hung

            declaration.

SIREN

Cui bono?
When they turned me into a bird, they
turned me into a woman,
                                        my top half full

of breasts and throat,
                                        the bottom, all claw

and dirty venom.

Partitioned like a nation,
so that I may sing
under the condition.

                                        If I could sing without condition,
I would give up singing.

                        Goals for a Monday:
                        —rip out the knees of the patriarchy
                        —practice histrionic but alluring singing
                        —do laundry

Having a voice demands
constant reparation.

                                        No one cares if you're
                                        half-beast, if you've got
                                        a great rack.

                                        Nothing saves a man like the pop
of a good braining.

Our song was a series of warnings,
which they took
to be pretty.

AMPHISBAENA

As pride swallows lust
              opening its jaws to 180 degrees.

Two-headed ouroboros
              makes itself a ring,
              mailed—rolling ...

                        The amphisbaena has no natural predators, being
                        unnatural. Lust overlaps chastity,

bronze scales on a sealed ring.

VULTURE

Better the fleshy crest of the Andean condor flapping like a torn ear,

                                the corpse's liquid slithering
                                off the slickness. Better to look

grand from a distance. Inside the bestiary, a music box with a figurine lathed
like my mother's mother
of a tragedy.

Life is an acid, feasting.

                                My father's corpse draped

like a legacy. I have burnt
his terror
in effigy.

OURANUS

As increment kills chaos, time also

regular measure

                to be supplanted by the yearn to blur
                faith's enriched
                oblivion   no mean horizon   no

unexpected jet as to be rent

                by one's own project   progression

cast as patricide

                the past at last
                perfected: cut

and met by that primordial wet net.
As Rhea, indifferent to time's arranged

                mind, buries vulnerability beyond

sickle, scythe, and mouth

                in the (whet) carved out.

KRONOS

—to the beginning—
          —birthed
          —absent father/happy childhood
          —adoptive maternal grandparents
          —eaten
          —bloody teens
          —adulthood
                    —>adulthood
                              —>>adulthood

SNOW GOOSE

Some tales are so attenuated that you can't feel what's happening: a girl with bad skin convinces her parents to buy her an expensive pair of jeans. Some lives are marked by a paucity of tragedy. One can assume that everyone suffers, though there are two kinds of difficulty: the kind you can speak about—your father's death, a crappy job, busting your Achilles—and others that entail the fear of being tapped again as aberrant. Let's say there was a young girl, so _____ that once she hit puberty, her mother put her in a glass carriage with a beast, a monster with a man's brain, face, and hands and the matted pelt and girth of a fire-breathing lion. After raping the girl, the beast reverts to his skinny, grimacing human form, dumping the girl's body in a field before driving the carriage home to the girl's mother who is immensely relieved to see the man come home in one piece. The girl will never forget the look on the man's face as he grabbed her small body, the look of sadistic pleasure as he twisted her small breast. The girl crawls into a well where she finds the skin of a large goose, which she puts on to cover her shame, cuts, and bruises. The skin zips up like a snowsuit, covering her from throat to toes in white feathers.

Crawling out of the well, the girl happily discovers her horse who had trotted after the carriage through the dark Woods, faithfully following the girl, patiently waiting for the girl to climb out of the well and into the night. The girl takes the horse's reins and walks beside it. They walk and walk, the girl in her loose suit of feathers that will tighten as she grows older, the horse occasionally stopping to eat grass, until they come upon a small cottage with one window lit up by firelight. Clutching the reins, the Goose-girl knocks at the door.

"Who is it at this time of night?" says a middle-aged man as he swings the door open. He is pleasantly surprised to see the girl, whom he takes to be an idiot, and her bright-eyed horse. He thinks they will do. His wife agrees.

His wife says, "You must be starving. I know your mother. You'll sleep in the barn and work for us in the morning."

When the girl awakes, she finds that her horse has been decapitated, its head hung up above the barn door. It is talking to her through its bleeding mouth and neck. It says:

"Don't be afraid. The worst has happened. Ten more years of servitude, followed by a decade of misery, retreat, and finally the turn. Half your life will be over, but you'll know when the spell is over, and the rest will feel like a boon, more life than you can now fathom. You'll return to your mother's cottage, her husband dead of natural causes. There's no grasping some people's motives. Your mother was always more childish than wicked. She will expect you to care for her."

The abandonment and severed head are pure fantasy. In the reality, the Goose-girl had to go home right after being raped. She had to live with the beast, who never touched her again, and her mother, working for them, going to school, eating their food, sleeping in their cottage. She won't remember her mother's role—throwing her into the carriage in spite of the girl's protests—until 20 years later. "I knew you would bring him back," explained the mother.

The girl will work 30 jobs before she is 21, sending her mother money from college. She will be a very good daughter, and then she won't be when she chooses, as the dead horse predicted, to be a person instead of a very competent erasure.

If the mother had said, "I never should have forced you to go," it would have made a difference. How does the grown hybrid, the woman/animal wearing her own skin, let go of the desire to be seen by the child who is an old woman? Is it like the skin of an animal that can be slipped off or more like the first undoing when the child becomes a woman?

"I knew a monster once," said the Duck to the Swan and the Goose. The Swan picked at a gnat on her pretty black neck.

"Yeah, right," said the Goose shifting her webbed orange feet. They were all sick of the Duck's melodrama, his flair for hogging the conversation with his real and imagined experiences.

"But I did," said the Duck. "He had a man's face and hands but a lion's mane and hind feet and a dragon's tail."

"Dragons don't exist," said the Swan yawning.

"I'd take a dragon over a human," said the Goose suddenly remembering something.

BLUE MORPHO

Is it like signing up for more slaughter? The torturer left
the cell crying. Victory was surprisingly easy after all
those years of bullying, but it won't feel satisfactory
because there never was an apology, and now
the beast that birthed you is dead. Wisdom says
                    take what you've made and forget
the rest. How sad to have lived and left
so much animus. How startling to know that releasing the animal
was a rational action to pull the emotional
through the portal. I am writing this for the shattered
instant. You were the right child in the wrong
alley. Your shape took the split. The pattern
was greater than the individual hits
like a spell that enchants the sleeper and her whole castle.

                    I don't believe it for a second. I believe
what happened happened to a form that persists
within my dismantled adult, my vertical eye
                    that won't forget.   Forgetfulness is for the dead
                    returning to the living, not for the living
on the way to death.

Wisdom says the way out is empathy: hearing
                    the suffering of the man as he cuts you
a new mouth.
                                        Trauma is like judgment: a border
                              disarrayed and
difficult to conceive. One has to intuit that
                              wanting to wield the knife comes from a grip
more painful than the strip of sorrow
that animates the victim.
To understand one suffering, you must reach into the distance
blotted with brightness.

I forgive you to save my own neck.
I forgive you, because you are no longer here
to behave with kindness or obtuseness. I
forgive you because I didn't want to be
anyone's mother or daughter. I wish my parents had talked
to someone other than their own instincts. I wish they had had
the company of persons other than child-savants.
Today, I speak
another version: a sensible goal
for a person.

SEA PEN

The pearl finishes the mother.

elision. Your spinneret has muffled

to escape history. I was an animal

understand what are the humans.

The sea fluttered like an asthmatic

another gland. After the family:

This is a homily on the snake's

my markings. I've been so fortunate

stuffed in a rumen. I smelled you to

I began with a handful of pupa.

candle. At the heart of the phylum,

the genus, the species.

ENGLISH MOLE

To push and push with raw pink claws like
hands of shin. To tunnel my love through wet
Earth, wet stars—no one needs the underneath
like me. To patrol the worm-drench of
my thinking. To bite a worm's head and cure
the rest as cache. Your flesh, my flesh, your dead
as dead, buried like a feeling. To push through
that wet, a scrum of worms whittling
my skin like a premonition. To have pushed
mountains into hills, ragged sooth from the
slid wall of healing. "Nothing,"
said the suicide, "is as sad as recovery."
To work myself forward like a noun or an entry.

BLACKBIRD

To be common and generally beneficial, warm like privacy, and dead. The blackbird rests between the rose lamp and the *American Heritage Dictionary* relaxed open on its wooden stand to botulism/bourn   bourn/box, the black ball of the blackbird's eye open and unmoving like a dab of gray-black roe. The blackbird's eye is the only light, the only thing not moving in the antechamber of learning. The blackbird's flesh is light as a feather, bound up upon the surface of the small wooden table tucked under the stairs, an inner eaves.

During the long afternoon of water and words, we forget about the blackbird on the table beneath the pencil sharpener, above the row of *Encyclopedia Britannica* wrapped in faded blue and dull dark gold. It is not until evening that we remember her, passing the dinner bell and tilting candelabra, the shallow fountain, carved fauns, and portraits of the munificent deceased. We climb the broad red case, past eyeless busts to the small table of morning, the blackbird's body now flown or gone.

2

Time flies like an arrow. Fruit flies like a banana.

ANTHONY OETTINGER

BUPLEURUM WANDERING CHAMBER

In the chamber of the wanderers, I was fourth in line.
Between the vial and the snow and the boot-print in the snow.
Smart, how they placed me in the double-walled chamber.
Smart, how this wood marks nothing like privacy.

Face in the cradle, I awake from a fallow dream.
Once was butcher paper waxing aqueous rhythm.
Someone sunk a hole where my face should have been.
Meanwhile in the chamber, boot-steps shuffle in.

Young doctor from Guangdong pulls rods from my back.
Shuts them in a red can labeled *liberation*.
His hands, two valves siphoning my bliss.
Once again, I shall drool empathically supine

in the wandering of the chamber at the stroke of the sign.

CEILING CRACK

This elegant white-on-white ceiling crack runs six and a half inches north-to-south and three and a quarter inches east-to-west to form what in some languages is an "L." The more conventionally attractive horizontal bar of the crack features a delicate cross-hatch pattern of plaster patching, while the more subtly appealing vertical portion is best described as the puffy spot. The crack accents an otherwise drab mid-century ceiling by slowly but surely reverting to its former glory as an exposed ceiling flap, notable for its glue-brown interior. Expertly covered up in 2004, the crack has been fixed sporadically since first being observed in 1963 and is currently widening at a pace of 20 mm per year, the same rate at which geologists believe North America is drifting away from the European Continent.

A note about availability: This crack is available for purchase for $2.83 billion dollars per day. The item is currently attached to a daisy-yellow Wallingford five-plex, which may or may not accompany the purchase. A larger crack may also be available (see below).

BASEMENT WALL CRACK

This Etruscan-style basement wall crack recalls the mysterious kohl-rimmed eyes of Theban princes depicted on some first-century BC urns. At five feet and three inches, the vertical crack spans the height of a squat, nefarious despot accustomed to ruling doe-eyed beauties with a jewel-encrusted twitch. Though long since surpassed by the technical innovations of Athenian and Hellenistic crack-makers, the anonymous creator of this crack ranks among the best of the Archaic period. The deceptively casual execution of this item belies the maker's conceptual egress, as the application of black, rubberized sealant to the crack's surface clearly serves as an allegory for the inscrutable, compliant nature of all those dark-haired people in other lands.

A note about availability: While such Orientalist pap is rare in basements, anyone wanting to buy it deserves what they get. It's a crack, and you can't have it.

STAIRWELL, PANAMA HOTEL

A potted palm at either end, as you rise upon the carpet in the dark, up the expectedly brown wooden stairs, brown like anticipation, which is a smell. The well is wide, and you walk in the middle to avoid touching the banister, because it reminds you of school, bachelor janitors, sliding along the metal rail under an old oak tree. Of course, each flight is identical to the one before: rounding each landing to greet an enormous silver bell, its hairy black wires to nowhere, hoping no one will see you, and below that eye-level on the wall, a framed sign reading FIRE ESCAPE in green capital letters, green like a noble gas, the sign itself laminated, tan, stained. Each sign bears an arrow piercing the two words, the kind of arrow that gets stuck in a tree. Each arrow pointing always to the right, to the end of the corridor past the dark brown doors slit shut like eyes, to the end, which is a pane, large and clean, painted neatly with the words FIRE ESCAPE in green capital letters, not peeling so much as scratched by the cracked finger of an imported Chinese. Who made our canal? This is the Americas, and past the window lies a black iron escape. The final flight smells of lemons, and when you hear a man and a woman talking above, you know she will approach you in a black velvet dress to ask if you are a guest. Imagine being the first to break dirt into ocean. Imagine doing this twice, because some President wants to make a place where two oceans meet. You will have to say no. The year is 1903.

A note about availability: This is an isthmus, and you've forgotten your hat.

HIRAM M. CHITTENDEN LOCKS, FISH LADDER VIEWING WINDOW #5

Built in 1976, the fish ladder's last window is best seen in mid-winter, when the view remains unobstructed by migrating fish. Standing at the railing, one looks beyond the double pane, the condensation's bare streaks, the vertical burns of algae, and submerged neon lights at either side of the window to stare into the tank, blank save for moving water. Recessed into a concrete wall, the window could be installation art, but it is better. Upon gazing, one perceives that the tank's upper portion is metonym for the firmament itself. As with the king's crown, the boiling cloud issuing forth from a square-cut portal to the ladder's next step inevitably recalls something bigger, and here it is the heavens pocked with rolling stars. The watery cloud boils backward out of its hole against the way of all flesh, which must always move across and down. Meanwhile, bits of light also break off the dark bottom to wobble through the blue murk up and to the left, approaching the surface like drunk moths. In the 21-step ladder, the window occupies the 18th rung. However, in the Ptolemaic system, it is the eighth heaven, also known as, "Pite, whiche may wele be called the firmament of perfeccyon, for it is the stablysshment of all holy conuersacyon, whereby man ... discerneth waters from waters." (W. de W., 1531)

A note about availability: She whosoever can discerneth the waters from the waters may purchase thise iteme for a Bicentennial mug, 16 tall ships, and a doubloon. She muste also be prepared to answere the question "But where are the fishe?" for as longe as she may live.

PATISSERIE DU MONDE

Because I am the nailbed and the bed of nails.
Because I am the pink and the char around the warm.
Because luck folds the lamb, and the luck unfolding ho.
Because I fingered two plums, and the plumber ate one.
Because crass craves company, and the candle kindles some of me.
Because I am the fifth, no fifth in line.
Because five said *make me seven,* and seven tied a rope.
Because I am the unsigned covenant, and a coven well, a coven.
Because line 10 marks exasperation, and 10 numbers sigh *Oh?*

As if music swam like number, numbing the bottom half.
As if geometry chased a note. As if a figment of a ghost.
As if flavor staved the hung, as if well flaved a flay.
As if beauty marked a question, the question parting low.
As if rusty made a shiny. And shiny antidote.

HK RULES THE PLANET

I, the big kitty they call Hello, was about to dream.
A cookie dream, as my sister the flat one
used to say, stashing it in the blue garden,
under the pink bottle we kept for picaresque.

Poor Mimi. Always baking. Right-side ribboned,
so recessed. It must be hard to be my twin star.
Sometimes, I still slip her my empties, the milk-colored ones,
the ones for whom moonlight speckled the precipice.

Mind the gap, they whisper. *Mind the gap.*

BALLAD OF THE SMALL DOG

Put up a paw and perk your ears,
my furred and flat-nosed friends.
Tis time to belly down and hear
my tale of baneful ends.

You may not know my origins
on planet BK9,
birthed in a grove of astral quince,
blue plums, and hand-shaped vines.

My mum taught me to teleport
from BK9 to Earth
when I was but a wee bairn squirt.
I was her favorite from the first.

Haha hahaha grrr grrr bone—
excuse me, mates, I've got
an itch—this biodome's
so dry. I've got a spot

that makes me growl and sigh,
but back to my smell-good yarn:
Brave backs, do be still. My
tale will make you turn

your noses on like being drawn
to a fragrant bole.
        There lived a dog of middling brawn
        but with brains of solar gold

who ruled a little cottage on
the edge of the bright Moon's

sea. She had two persons:
a woman and her son.

One day, the son with dark black hair
sailed away on the long-burnt
lunar sea to where
no soul sails, unless it wants

to be alone for ere, a sense-
less concept to you and we,
but there's no kenning humans
and their hairless needs.

The boy's mum knew precisely where
he'd gone. She'd rued her son
in advance, knowing her dear
odd child's ambitions

to be gone, erased, chalked
up to the sweet Moon's ether.
She mourned his loss through nightly walks
with her faithful friend and keeper.

Lads and Lasses, I said my song
would make you howl and sniff.
Tis time to sit among
ourselves and lick the ones we're with.

3

Even though a tiger is biting you,
if you gain consciousness (you can) live.

KOREAN PROVERB

FABLESQUE

Now gather up the elements: sleep and kiss
and fat and hair. Get me a goose and glass
a casket. Tump a princeling full of blare.
Here is the fish blown to ocean. Here,

the little basket of bittering flares.
Silver and silver, sighs the mirror.
Silver, silver, hi-dee-ho. Under each story
lies a fable, beneath the fable, a shallow

row. I put on white to stave the worry.
My lips are as red as nuclear snow.
Bring me a cup of explicable fury.
Divine the whither, if not the when.

I toss a coin in the seven-cent fountain.
The mirror tells me: *Wish again.*

TROPIQUE DU MAL

Night again, and I lie awake among
the blunt consumptions of flesh to flesh,
air creased with the reticulate slur and hum
of wings, moths bursting from mint-pressed
sacs. How tenderly their mouths tear at the light.
My love, this hammock is not what it seems;
I swing from pole to pole knowing nothing is right.
My fingers wrap a palm's anchored beam,
as fever gifts me with a rave payola.
Again, I will not dream. I will not let
this harbor break me. I will hold the halo
that holds these hands, shuddering soft black heat.
I will let them all strum this deciduous strip
of a heart, desiring nothing: not love, not sleep.

THE BEAUTIFUL PLACES

I was 18, traveling alone, when a wise
woman told me: The beautiful places
always preserve. Beauty, she said, belies
consistently conventional choices,
and social progress only happens in the gray
and dreary climes. She lived in London;
she was dissing Italy, the southern U.S.A.
And while the theory occurs to me again,
I have to say I think beauty is merely
overrated. I'm in Colorado, staring morosely
at the cheeses in the town's only grocery
thinking: *Cracker Barrel or Kraft?* A manky
blonde muttering *foreigner* scuts on by.
I'm an adult. *Lovely,* I think and let it fly.

BLOW BLOW BLOW

I was the girl cried Wolf eat me. I was
the girl cried Wolf, hey don't eat me. I was
the girl cried woof, cried girl, cried Wolf, cry. I,
like a little baby said, OK, bye.

I was the girl misunderstammering.
Wuh was the girl cried gimme *mot mot mot.*
Was the hot Wolf having a summer fling.
Was the girl cried, Oh, Piggy, Oh, Oh, Oh …

Now you know every tale is a dirty
little lie designed to dupe the lovely
and the meek, those who might lack the wordy

predilections that you and I possess.
The one with the teeth thinks he will take me.
What happens next is anyone's guess.

THE FROG-PRINCE

"You're just like every toad I've ever met,"
 said the Princess to her smooth companion.
"Except maybe more persistent," she thought
 quietly. "I'm still not sure why a person

like me should bother with a totally slimy,
web-footed *thing,* when I'm so perfectly
content with my ball and myself." "I see,"
said the frog laconically. "Perfectly

content." Something about his tone—half-burp,
so sure—instantly enraged the Princess, who
grabbed the frog's slick carapace and threw

it at a wall, which broke the beast into
his handsome, manly origins. "How warped,"
said the plussed Princess. "Now what do I do?"

THE GOLDEN AGE

AFTER A LINE BY JUDAH ADASHI

Why pretty man no smile? If I were
as beautiful as you, I surely would
not be so glum. No, no. If I had your
round-eye, infant blues and Afghan blood

or whatever genetic mix makes you look goy,
I'd touch myself all over two or three
times a day, and I would thoroughly enjoy
the company. Yes, yes. Indeed. *Mais oui.*

I am as beautiful as you and maybe
even a tiny bit more. So now you know
how I spend my time. Perhaps we should

make some cute little hapa babies,
but only if we can do this in vitro,
since sex is untidy and also you're married.

BABY DADA

The day before the day before the day
before Xmas, and I'm pushing the pram
of someone else's baby girl. Live eyes
in a live head, but the body is dumb

mechanics: this babe's a bot or half-
bot as it were, and I'm not sure which part
is more disturbing—the lubricious tuft
with its talking red mouth or the open heart

spilling its tubular guts, all fake for
the taking. Also, she's the size of a child,
way too large to be encarriaged, her
enormous limbs—flesh or plastic—piled

like hair. The infant's mother has disappeared.
She's all mine, this hybrid, totally weird.

SALT LAKE

AFTER BORIS MIKHAILOV

"Let's face it," says Marko. "We're from a hole
six inches deep." "OK," I say, bobbing
agreeably, leaking a bit. We roll
another big cigar and watch the hobbling

Moon drag her claws above the sky. I scratch
my back and add, "Well, actually I don't
have parents. I formed psychotically in a patch
of flavored paste." "Ah," he sighs like a punt.

This makes me furious of course, but that's
just Marko. Once, I told him how I ran
into his father at the lake. Some bats

made off with his lunch, as he dribbled on
into a creek. "Let's not talk about the past,"
said M. "Childhood's a finger on a note."

LATE CAESURA

Beauty and the beast of it—the best of
the beast, the rest of the beast being S.
The dram or drip of it, the slovenly
bod, caprice or nod yes, no, yes.   Good

F it. Had it—strung profit
and make the burst of it. Pardon the X.
Spit logic and totally full of it—
—like it or knot. Get on it. Abet

set deficit—spit habit out of sheer
intuit but not that into it—er—
make a bed of it—

er—I meant it—
R, so be it, R,
damn sobriquet—brick it. Break.

THE GRAY BOX

The apple is red, because the leaves are
green. There's a place in the brain for orange, a
grove of reception like Nebraska or
Rome. Everyone is fond of Iowa.

The moving dot is where the monkey steers
his vision. The macaque's thoughts click like a
warm clock. Color induction: mirror error
of the mind's eye. On the brain's map, orange may

be next to red, as one might hope or not.
The monkey's thinking is a bouncing box.
The apple is red, because the leaves are not.
The fruit must be seen to be plucked, though tex-

ture has another channel known to us as touch.
There's a woman with four cones in her mind's watch.

THE YELLOW BOX

Dear Confucius, do I look sallow?
Double helix besmirches the bee's knees.
What the canary, koi, and lion know.
The cell where she set little women free.

The Queen's battalion after taking losses.
Identical and therefore expendable.
With gravity and joy as their witnesses.
The future smoking like a signal.

The journalist's fever is in the lab.
A stain imprinted on the teeth of nation.
The dragon's store wrapped by the dragon's lip.
Hammer, fin, streak, pine, jack, stone, cake, rain.

Sky-candle rendered. Farewell, orb. Bye, gas.
The triangle and diamond meet their match.

THE RED BOX

Shift is the shade between gray and detection,
warm and flooded as redemption, burnt
semantic and dry. Ash is the wax of vermillion,
a drip in the Emperor's robe of gold. Rose turns

the Empress' throat, her crown of poison oak.
Extensions russet, twice revoked, are silt
to slather heart's doors. Heart must never look
for more. Pure luck is ruby's shining tilt:

Invisible salute to one and one.
From brick to smudge and on again. From cask
to trunk and orange-red. Crimson as a bone.
Engine fires engine, dusk to dusk.

Incarnadine is doubled vision, carmine to
the touch: a slip in an eight-sided knot.

NUDE PALETTE

What a muse, what a mess, this state of undress
descending the spiral stare—to look back is
to profess, resume the harness, and lose
the myth of progress—save us and tear us

apart to finesse this duress, stress by mis-
step. Give me access or emptiness—
the world is my terrace—
an embarrassment of purchase, promise—

Hello, virtuoso! You had me at emo.
I was dead as a dodo, a solo
soprano with a face for radio
and a case of mono, working *pro*

bono for the *ecce homo.* Show me the jello
en masse, in toto. Oh, no. Say yes.

CELESTIAL SCALE

Is it a falling tune or human time,
this all-in-one paradigm I'm happening?
Is it a reeling in or common crime,
this whaling ton of feeling underpinning

this veiling, un- of quelling tally up?
Feeling one heart beat under weather, feeling
sun on the chilling station of this pop
'n' mom operation, sailing on, telling

one clap and hum, snap and chime after another.
Is it an open home or flip and sell
I'm dealing in? This swelling bun, proper
sum, kneeling down, map and climb of calling

forth in dueling din, anodyne and crimson
boom, shelling in, and peeling hymn, *om, um.*

ORIGIN STORY

The gods of Inertia, Entropy, and Delay
sat down to a round of three-way chess.
"After you," said Inertia decorously. "Nay,"
replied Entropy, swaying her gross mass

for emphasis. "I went first the last
time we played; it's Delay's turn to begin."
"Ugh," said Delay. "I hate this game. Why test
my patience? You both know I can't imagine

a worse way to spend the day than to loll
around an artificial grid sacrificing
castle- and horse-shaped minutes for your mental

indulgence. Plus the Queen has too many
armaments." "OK," said Inertia, placing
a heavy hand on Delay. "Don't be whiny."

SONNET TWO

AFTER WILLIAM SHAKESPEARE

Pumped as a golden animal or
breast full of dark light
mineral, let the furrow
of forty winters

lapse. For a season,
did I wax
the tallow. Let
the wane begin.

For forty summers too,
did I hie
my prime and hem
my love to

those zones above and fix
my star.

ASTRAL SONNETS

1

Geometry and the Moon creatures chased
a beautiful orange. His round mounded
lips eclipsed all reminiscences of home.
Earth (for her part) cast in the appointed
lineup three halves whose shadows stream-surfaced
like two at the end of the world. Wound and wounded
to see his wounded side. Deep-worshipped comb.

Geometry and the Moon's animal disjointed.
As it was foretold: dipped and then blessed.
To gather a creature mythological, grounded.
To hold the undivided, to everlast, to roam.
Earth, for her part, cast at the anointed
her hour, her lot with the voice-dripped honey.
His shadow of Sol or Mani (of Mani).

2

Thirteen-thirteen that may be 39
interpretations, but their relative
holes indicate another black sample.

All data malleable in the midst
of perfect sources, as determined by
his spectral dark remnants whose neural shine

gives up analysis. Indicative
because was drawn along with the normal
solar masses. Better to have been blitzed

by perfect sources. As determined by
her dark spectral remnants whose virile ion
sang collective.
                    Divided spiral
                              and its neutron.

3

Studded with broad wonders, scopic objects
in the sky command the Southern. This
region, having given birth, projects
cluster: Deep Sky. Minutes to see what else

round region holds, the region round the Tra-
pezium star. From sparkling, use
telescopes, binoculars, and awe.
And can easily chew up, if you choose

the lower left sky as darkness pause.
As the passive, the five planets, as
mesmerizing as it may be, as
at least a few bright swirls of gas,

and even Sirius
                        and even the mass—

4

To dodge these deadly molecular clouds,
rip these shedding a small red star in-
to the witnessed. In principle, we might see
a perfect ring, the Sun's age, countless other

open clusters that exceed objects.
Indeed. Most giant far from the galactic,
the destruction galaxy at large. [A]
But the galaxy would need, so inhabit the in-

ner galaxy. However relentlessly giant,
twenty or so will be shining still
irregular. If the two objects in
the outer Milky (in the outer Milky),

if the galaxy is the slightest, chances are
a barred spiral, elliptical, chances are a

NOTES

In writing the beastly poems, I read numerous medieval bestiaries, as well as nonfiction books on animals for adults and children including: *Bestiary: An Illuminated Alphabet of Medieval Beasts* by Jonathan Hunt, *The Medieval Menagerie: Animals in the Art of the Middle Ages* by Janetta Rebold Benton, *Animal Encyclopedia* by Dorling Kindersley, *The Marvels of Animal Behavior* published by the National Geographic Society, *The Kingfisher Illustrated Animal Encyclopedia, Monster Myths: The Truth About Water Monsters* by Staton Rubin, *Animals in Translation* by Temple Grandin and Catherine Johnson, and *The Illustrated Compendium of Amazing Animal Facts* by Maja Säfström. I also spent many pleasant hours perusing the Rosenbach Museum & Library's edition of Comte de Buffon's *Histoire Naturelle, générale et particulière, avec la description du Cabinet du Roi* and the Rosenbach's trove of Marianne Moore's correspondence, drafts of poems, and clippings about animals in the news.

In retelling the Greek myths of Ouranus and Kronos, I drew upon several sources, including the *Apollodorus: The Library of Greek Mythology,* translated and with an introduction and notes by Robin Hard. In referencing the fairy tales, I reread an old, beloved copy of *Grimm's Fairy Tales Illustrated* published by the Airmont Publishing Company, *Jacob and Wilhelm Grimm: Selected Tales,* translated by Joyce Crick, and many other collections.

The epigraph that opens the second section has been attributed, probably erroneously, to Groucho Marx, the originator of other witty aphorisms concerning animals and humans. The likely author of this quotation is Anthony Oettinger, a mid-20th-century computer scientist and early investigator of artificial intelligence. The two sentences test a machine's ability to discern between different parts of speech.

The "Interiors" poems were commissioned for a special issue of *ARCADE: Architecture and Design in the Northwest* focusing on objects and architectural features found in interiors. I came across the quotation attributed to W. de W., 1531 under the "firmament" entry in *The Compact Edition of the Oxford English Dictionary* (Oxford University Press, 1971).

"Salt Lake" takes its cue from Boris Mikhailov's 1986 photographic series of sunbathers and swimmers in a Ukrainian lake fed by industrial pollution. The photographic series *Salt Lake* was published by Steidl.

"The Gray Box" draws upon the research of neurobiologist and painter Bevil Conway.

"Astral Sonnets" is a cut-up collage poem using old issues of *Scientific American* as the source text.

ACKNOWLEDGMENTS

Many thanks to the editors of the following publications, who previously published these poems, sometimes under different titles:

amberflora
  "Bear" and "Ursus"

ARCADE: Architecture and Design in the Northwest
  Interiors: "Ceiling Crack," "Basement Wall Crack," "Stairwell, Panama Hotel," and "Hiram M. Chittenden Locks, Fish Ladder Viewing Window #5"

Bennington Review
  "Siren" and "Blue Morpho"

Better Magazine
  "The Gray Box"

Black Clock
  "Fablesque"

Borderlands: Texas Poetry Review
  "Tropique du Mal" and "The Beautiful Places"

Cranky Literary Journal
  "Patisserie du Monde"

ENTROPY
  "Antelope," "Amphisbaena," and "Snow Goose"

Exquisite Corpse
  "Astral Sonnets"

Fence
  "HK Rules the Planet"

Gargoyle Magazine
  "Origin Story"

The Gihon River Review
  "Baby Dada"

Green Mountains Review
  "The Ants"

GUEST
    "Kronos" and "Ballad of the Small Dog"

The Harvard Gazette
    "The Frog-Prince"

Jet Fuel Review
    "Termite" and "Vulture"

jubilat
    "Heliconius Melpomene" and "The Golden Age"

Mobile City
    "Blow Blow Blow"

New Delta Review
    "Rabbit" and "Wolf"

No Tell Motel
    "Bupleurum Wandering Chamber"

Poetry
    "English Mole"

Poetry Northwest
    "Maiden," "Sea Pen," and "Blackbird"

St. Petersburg Review
    "Salt Lake"

Tupelo Quarterly
    "Ouranus"

Unsplendid
    "The Yellow Box" and "Celestial Scale"

Upstart: A Journal of Renaissance Studies
    "Sonnet Two"

The Volta
    "Late Caesura"

"The Frog-Prince" was reprinted in *250 Poems: A Portable Anthology*, 3rd edition, edited by Peter Schakel and Jack Ridl (Bedford/St. Martin's) and *Approaching Literature: Reading,*

Thinking, Writing, 4th edition, edited by Peter Schakel (Bedford/St. Martin's).

Much gratitude to Rachel Levitsky, Krystal Languell, Rachael Wilson, James Loop, and everyone at the Belladonna* Collaborative for publishing the chapbook *Hello, virtuoso!* in which "The Red Box" and "Nude Palette" first appeared and for their vital work supporting women writers.

I would also like to thank Elizabeth E. Fuller, the librarian at the Rosenbach Museum & Library for facilitating my animal-themed research there.

Thank you to the Radcliffe Institute for Advanced Study, the Corporation of Yaddo, Djerassi Resident Artists Program, Kunstnarhuset Messen, and Fundación Valparaíso for providing me with space, time, funding, and fellowship—all crucial to the making and reshaping of these poems. Many thanks also to Bennington College, Ursinus College, and the University of Pennsylvania for supporting the writing, revision, and submission of this book, with special thanks to Becky Jaroff, Julia Bloch, and Veronica Jorgensen, and to my brilliant and wonderful students at all of those institutions.

My deepest appreciation to Aimee Nezhukumatathil for selecting this collection for Tupelo Press's Berkshire Prize, to Kristina Marie Darling for her sharp, swift, and steady stewardship of the manuscript's evolution to book, and to Jeffrey Levine, David Rossitter, and everyone at Tupelo Press for their ebullient support. I am honored to be among Tupelo's authors.

Many thanks also to my fellow presenters on several Korean American feminist poetry panels (at the Associated Writers & Writing Programs Conference, the Split This Rock Poetry Festival, and the Thinking Its Presence: Race & Creative

Writing Conference at the University of Montana) whose conversations abetted this work: E. J. Koh, Marci Calabretta Cancio-Bello, Youna Kwak, Hannah Sanghee Park, Franny Choi, and Arlene Kim.

A million thank you's to So Yeon Kim for granting permission to feature her gorgeous artwork on the cover and to Amy Sillman for introducing me to So Yeon's work. Thank you, Kenji Liu, for the book's beautiful design.

To all of the following people who gave their energy to this work one way or another, my continued gratitude for your generosity and presence: David Lehman, Stacey Harwood-Lehman, Anna Lena Phillips Bell, Erin Malone, Shawn Wong, Alan Lau, Kazuko Nakane, Simone Muench, Caryl Pagel, Hilary Plum, Christine Hume, Jeffrey Di Leo, Lindsey Drager, Christy Davids, Zack Finch, Caren Beilin, Nabil Kashyap, Andrea Lawlor, Art Middleton, Joanna Ruocco, Jason Zuzga, Jessica Rae Bergamino, Sarah Richards Graba, Reb Livingston, Christina Davis, Janice Lee, Jason Snyder, John Cleary, Kristine Leja, Sarah Mangold, Rebecca Woolf, Ida Stewart, Douglas Basford, Jason Gray, Dora Malech, Lesley Wheeler, Martha Silano, Elizabeth Senja Spackman, Diana Whitney, Don Mee Choi, Martha Silano, Charles Mudede, Christopher Frizzelle, Deborah Woodard, Dave Karp, David Groff, John Keene, Michael Snediker, Maureen McLane, Daphne Brooks, Matt Jacobsen, Taylor Davis, Diana Sorensen, Nick Turse, Barbara Weinstein, Irene Lusztig, Miki Lusztig, Don Berman, Meredith Grass, Jessica Lowenthal, Kenna O'Rourke, Tracey Cravens-Gras, Suzanne Buffam, Heather McHugh, Marla Akin, Ingunn van Etten, Vanessa Lyon, Heather Vermeulen, Emily Weissbourd, Lindsay Higdon, Steve Factor, Clay Smith, Martin Wilson, Perry Sayles, Steve Harvey, Pam Thurschwell, Ragnhild Jåstad Vågen, Ingeborg Jåstad Røyset, Marjorie LaRowe, Allen Shawn, Jean Randich, Jill Moser, Anne Thompson, Matt Saunders, Katarina Burin, Mary Ruefle,

Michael Burkard, Stephen Shapiro, Christopher Wendell Jones, Ann Yi, Mario D'Souza, James Hannaham, Rosa Alcalá, Sunny Kim, and Brodie Sattva Hong.

And to Joanna Klink, David Micah Greenberg, and Liz Powell, a world of gratitude for your expert counsel and enduring friendship—this book would not be what it is without you, and you have made all of my books and my life better.

Photo credit: Stephanie Mitchell

Anna Maria Hong is the author of the novella *H & G* (Sidebrow Books), winner of the A Room of Her Own Foundation's Clarissa Dalloway Prize; and *Age of Glass*, winner of the Cleveland State University Poetry Center's First Book Poetry Competition and the Poetry Society of America's 2019 Norma Farber First Book Award. Her second poetry collection, *Fablesque*, won Tupelo Press's Berkshire Prize. A former Bunting Fellow at the Radcliffe Institute for Advanced Study, she has published poetry and fiction in over 70 journals and anthologies, including *The Nation, The Iowa Review, Harvard Review, Poetry Daily, Best New Poets*, and *The Best American Poetry*.

RECENT AND SELECTED TITLES
FROM TUPELO PRESS

Slick Like Dark (poems) by Meg Wade

Arrows (poems) by Dan Beachy-Quick

Took House (poems) by Lauren Camp

Shahr-e-jaanaan: The City of The Beloved (poems) by Adeeba
Shahid Talukder

The Nail in the Tree: Essays on Art, Violence, and Childhood (essays/
visual studies) by Carol Ann Davis

Exclusions (poems) by Noah Falck

Lucky Fish (poems) by Aimee Nezhukumatathil

Butterfly Sleep (drama) by Kim Kyung Ju, translated by Jake Levine

Canto General: Song of the Americas (poems) by Pablo Neruda,
translated by Mariela Griffor with Jeffrey Levine, Nancy Naomi
Carlson, and Rebecca Sieferle

Franciscan Notes (poems) by Alan Williamson

boysgirls (hybrid fiction) by Katie Farris

Diurne (poems) by Kristin George Bagdanov

America that island off the coast of France (poems) by Jesse
Lee Kercheval

Epistle, Osprey (poems) by Geri Doran

Hazel (fiction) by David Huddle

What Could Be Saved: Bookmatched Novellas & Stories (fiction) by
Gregory Spatz

Native Voices: Indigenous American Poetry, Craft and Conversation
(poetry and essays) CMarie Fuhrman, Dean Rader, editors

The Book of LIFE (poems) by Joseph Campana

Dancing in Odessa (poems) by Ilya Kaminsky

Fire Season (poems) by Patrick Coleman

Xeixa: Fourteen Catalan Poets (poems) edited by Marlon L. Fick and Francisca Esteve

At the Gate of All Wonder (fiction) by Kevin McIlvoy

Flight (poems) by Chaun Ballard

Republic of Mercy (poems) by Sharon Wang

At the Drive-In Volcano (poems) by Aimee Nezhukumatathil

Feast Gently (poems) by G. C. Waldrep

Legends of the Slow Explosion: Eleven Modern Lives (biographical essay) by Baron Wormser

See our complete list at tupelopress.org